Your 60 Minute Lean Gov't

The Lean Government Handbook

Your 60 Minute Lean Government

The Lean Government Handbook

January 2016

First Edition

ISBN: **978-1523310937**

Also by Jason Tisbury:

7 Steps To A Lean Business

Pocket Happiness

Your 60 Minute Lean Business

- 5S
- Total Productive Maintenance
- Kaizen Mindset
- Standarised Work
- Just in Time
- Jidoka

Compilations:

Your 60 Minute Lean Business

- Volume 1 The Foundations
- Volume 2 The Pillars
- The Collection

Contents

Preface

In alignment with all of my earlier books, this guide is quite short; this is by design. My personal philosophy on lean education came about when I was undertaking my post graduate studies in Business at University. I was already well trained in lean through working with Toyota and through many years of trial and error (the University of the Real World), however was needing some formal qualifications. While researching lean through the University libraries I found just about every publication on lean to be oversized and full of waste. I found this quite frustrating and at the same time amusing as lean is all about removing waste; yet here was all of this waste!

I made a commitment to do my part in bringing the lean back into lean education and promptly wrote my first book "7 Steps To A Lean Business" as part of my final graded work. Seven books later and many thousands of sales I have brought my attention to this, my latest work.

Foreword

Can lean work in the public sector or is the private sector only to benefit from the lean systems and philosophies? I believe the methods of lean are a perfect fit for the public sector; in fact I believe the public sector can benefit more than any other, I will explain why.

First, let's discuss what the main benefits of a lean system are:

- Increased safety

- Improved customer satisfaction

- Increased efficiency

- Improved profitability

- Increased availability

These are a few of the benefits a lean system can help a business to realize. There are many more, both tangible and intangible; hard and soft.

In most of the above benefits, the goal is to reduce the overall operating costs of a business while increasing the revenue with a resultant increase in profits. That is a simple view of the hard benefits of lean. There are many more soft benefits including:

- Improved morale

- Reduction in waste

- Increased team work

- Breakdown of silo's

To realize the sustainable benefits of a lean system it is critical that the soft benefits are achieved. These are the real basis of lean. The hard benefits are simply the outcomes or results of the soft benefits. This fact is lost on many people, both believers and non-believers; and is a major reason many have the opinion that lean is best left to the private sector and has no place in the public sector. I disagree strongly and know that the soft benefits and the tangible hard benefits can be of great importance to the public sector and the community served by these organizations. Furthermore, I believe the real benefits of lean can make a significant difference to the way government organizations of all sizes and types can add value to the community.

Many employees of government organizations do have the very best intentions and may take offence to some of the generalizations contained in this book; this is not the intention. These same people are probably quite frustrated at how difficult the 'red tape' can make their job. This book will discuss many of these frustrations and show there is a better way.

This book is not about politics and will not discuss the differences in the major political parties or systems. The book also will not spout new or old political agenda's or my own personal views on politics. What is in this book can be achieved regardless of the politics (as long as there is a functioning democracy).

You may ask what qualifications do I have to write such a book; well as a lean and quality practitioner for over 20 years, I have applied the tools contained within these pages in many organizations across many industries from fashion, importing, exporting, printing, automotive, manufacturing, FMCG, food, construction and even public sector. Having written seven previous books on the subject of lean business systems, including the international best selling title "Your 60 Minute Lean Business 5S Implementation Guide" I spent a number of years applying lean in the Local Government sector while researching for this book; this time was a mixture of direct employment and consultation to a number of government organizations.

Rather than discussing what I found wrong with the current systems during this time, the approach I have taken in this book is to simply discuss how the implementation of lean systems can be applied in the public sector and how they will benefit the organization and the community (to prove points there will be a certain amount of rhetoric). I will be commencing the book with a discussion on the community. The community is an all-encompassing term to mean the people (customers, stakeholders, patrons, workers etc). I will be using the term 'organization' in this book as a reference to the community serving body e.g. Police, Government, School; in the context of this book 'organization' does not refer to a commercial operation.

1. The Community

In the commercial world the main objective of lean is to remove waste from the organizations processes in order to provide the highest value to the customers, thereby providing greater value than the competition in the market. This waste elimination becomes a competitive advantage.

A government organization strictly speaking is not a commercial operation and therefore its priority is not to gain a competitive advantage. This is not always the case, as many government agencies are in direct opposition with commercial businesses. We will be focusing on the agencies that provide essential services to the community; these services can be anything from Police, Fire, Health, Education, and Local Municipal. There are many more examples of such community focused government agencies but I'm sure you get the idea.

You may be thinking that all of the above examples are community focused already and you would be correct in most cases. The agencies themselves and the individuals employed are often designed to provide a service to the public and the original design intent often remains. In these times of commercialism and bonus incentives however, the methods and the objectives have become a little blurred (more than a little in some instances).

The whole idea of community engagement has gone by the wayside and has become a requirement that must be 'ticked off' rather than an important and valuable part of the process. By this I mean the process remains as a shell but the outputs are often low in value and meaning due to:

a) The process employed by the organization, and/or;

b) The disillusionment of the community in the process and the people.

Why is community engagement so important? Although community organizations are not and shouldn't try to be commercial operations, there are a number of areas they can learn from the commercial world. Look at the best commercial businesses around the world and there a number of obvious traits that all of them share. In isolation, none of these things make them successful however when combined into a management and operating system they do. One of these is they know who their customers are and what they want. They call it market research; in the world of community organizations we call it community engagement.

Remember, the community is both the shareholder and the customer of the organization (not really that dissimilar to many large publicly shared commercial operations). In the commercial world, if the customer isn't happy with the product they will not buy it, it's as simple as that. In the world of community organizations however, the customer doesn't always have a choice, they have to use the services or go without as there are no alternatives. In other circumstances they have no option to not use the service (or pay for the service whether they use it or not).

Let's take a look at a couple of common community organization types and their customers.

Police Service

The Police Service has 3 distinct customer groups.

1) Victims of crime or other incidents
2) The general public
3) The accused and criminals

These three customer groups have very diverse needs and even more different expectations from the service. The first group would expect the service to assist them in their time of need and bring the accused to justice.

The second group would have similar expectations as the first however probably less passionately as they may not have been aggrieved or had a crime committed against them.

The third group however will have very different expectations and needs. While they may hope the service turns a blind eye, their realistic expectations are likely to be fair treatment.

From all of these customers' points of view, they do not have any choice of service provider although some may wish they did. Whether the service is efficient and effective or not, the customer cannot choose an alternative other than during an election period.

Education

Let's now take a look at an education system; a publicly owned junior school. These may be called elementary, primary, junior; whatever the name it is the education facility of students under 12 years in most countries.

The customers of the facility are:

1) The students
2) The parents and guardians
3) The community
4) The teaching faculty

As in the previous example these four customer groups have overlapping yet unique expectations from the service. The students and parents will have specific educational expectations while the community will have more generic expectations regarding levels of education and the teaching of community values. The last groups' expectations will be to be provided with adequate tools and resources to provide the service they have trained for and to be accorded respect by their management team.

Unlike the first example, in most areas there are alternatives to the public education system. If any of the customers in groups one, two or four are not satisfied with the level of service received they have the opportunity to opt out and utilise the services of a private, commercial alternative. Those customers in the third group however cannot opt for an alternative as their needs are not specific, but are a general community expectation level.

As you can see from the above couple of examples, an organizations customers are diverse in many ways and unlike a commercial operation they are not usually able to choose which customer segment they want to service. Being a community organization, they usually have to deliver their services to all customers who choose to or have to use them. This does create some challenges for the organization as they need to design their services to suit a broad spectrum of users.

This brings us back to community engagement. To achieve the above it is imperative that the community is engaged in the design of the services. Yes, this is the responsibility of the organization to provide a method for community engagement however, it is also the community's (customers) responsibility to be engaged and provide feedback to help the organization help them. The customer should not refuse to be engaged in the design of the service and then later complain the service does not meet their expectations or needs. Remember, the customer is also the owner so they do have an opportunity at certain times and circumstances to have their input. The old saying "the rich get richer" is true; have you ever wondered why many government policies and services help the rich get richer? They have a voice and they use it to lobby and bring about change in a constructive manner. I don't mean going out and protesting or striking for a cause – this is not constructive – but going to the table with solutions to problems that also helps their own cause.

So the first step to achieving a lean government is for the community to engage in the:

- Service design
- Service implementation
- Regular feedback

- Election process

As part of the community if you take all of the above seriously, you will play your part in bringing about a better system.

2. The Organization

Now to the organization; obviously every organization is unique and every organization type is also unique. Although unique in purpose and structure, community based organizations all have one major similarity. Their objective is to provide an essential service to their community. There are many government organizations that do not appear to directly provide a service or product to the community; they are all part of a larger system.

Unlike a commercial operation, a community organizations objective is not to provide a profit to owners or shareholders. They are, or at least they set out to be not for profit in nature and provide a good value service to their customers. It is probably true that some have lost sight of their original objectives however most government organizations are still trying to deliver on their promise; they have lost their way and need to realign their services to their objectives and the communities needs. More on this in the next chapter...

For now let's discuss the typical challenges faced in all businesses but have a great impact on the value provided by governments. Because these challenges are not really any different from the challenges faced in the commercial world many of the tools and methods used will have the same impact when applied in a way to suit the unique requirements of a government type business unit. Some of these tools are explained in detail later in this book.

Challenge:

Misalignment of goals

This challenge is a big one for all businesses. I have worked in organizations on both sides of this challenge. When a business has aligned goals it is a sight to behold. This by far should be the number one goal for every leadership team. When accomplished, everything else seems simple and very achievable. Imagine a leadership team all working as one for the same objectives; no politics involved, no ego's just a team working as one. This is true synergy. This doesn't have to be a dream; I have seen it and lived it.

When it goes wrong a business can be strangled to a stop. Obviously there is a broad range of operating between perfection and stoppage; above I have described my experiences working with the best environment, now I will explain the times I have spent working in the worst environment. Unfortunately, probably like many of you I have spent more of my career working in bad environments than good, this is an indication of how few businesses get this right. My experiences in government have been negative unfortunately. When the goals are not aligned the leadership does not work together towards a common goal and there is likely to be a lot of politics played out in the office as leaders attempt to "get one up" on each other.

There doesn't need to be a winner and a loser; back in the 1990's the buzz term was "win/win". We seem to have forgotten that this can be a realistic and achievable outcome.

The impacts on a government business unit have a greater implication on the customers than that of a commercial operation. If a commercial business suffers from misaligned goals the customer will probably notice a decline in the customer service levels and move on to another service provider. In a government business this often isn't possible as we saw in the earlier chapter. For this reason the community suffers due to the inability of the leadership team to align the goals across the business. Some of the problem comes from the fact many government employees do have an altruistic ambition and are working to serve. This creates a level of determination to stick to their beliefs regardless of the organizational objectives; this can come across as ego driven but I believe it mostly is not. For these reasons it is both more critical and more difficult for a government organization to create and nurture aligned goals and objectives.

So how does a business achieve aligned goals? Regardless of the business type the same process is used and will be discussed at length in a later chapter. Effective business planning is the process and is a little different for different business types but effectively you are cascading the goals down through the business.

Challenge:

Resource restrictions: Cashflow, labour, equipment & tools

This is a very broad constraint that every business ever in existence has had to face throughout their journey, so is far from being unique to governments. All of the above restrictions result in the same outcome: a reduced or poor service being provided to the customer. It is very important to understand a critical point about lean:

Lean is not about doing more with less. This can be a result of deploying a good lean strategy but should not be the driving objective. Lean is primarily about providing only what the customer wants, when they want it, in the amount they want it i.e. eliminating waste from a business or business process. This is a critical understanding, many lean journey's fail due to a lack of understanding this single point. Remember, lean is about improving your customers experience and value; this is why lean is such a good fit with government departments.

Back to the challenge... A lack of resources can be a challenge that is difficult to overcome as it isn't always within your control (depending on the position you hold). The best approach to this problem is to not have the problem in the first place through better business planning; yes it comes back to business planning again. This will be explained further in a later chapter, but from my experiences working with government agencies, business planning is not a strong point. Simplified, business planning is a 3 step process.

1) Always start with a bottom up approach. Build up your budget recording everything you want to achieve and accomplish, including carry overs. Prioritise your goals.

2) Next perform a top down approach with the income and financials. Record all of the income you will achieve during the budget period including carry overs.

3) Overlay the two and determine which goals are achievable and those that are not by working down your priorities.

It is that simple, the process does take some time to complete across an entire organization but if you are making the process more complex you are probably not going to get it right.

What I have experienced when working with government departments has been diverse and usually omits one of the above steps. Either the second or third. When the second step is omitted the results can be one of two:

1) The department will not have sufficient funds to complete its goals and provide a service that meets the customers' expectations.

2) The department will have surplus funds at the end of the budget period; this may seem like a good thing, however when a government departments sole objective is provide a service to the community, making a profit is not absolutely necessary; planned savings for future projects is necessary (planned savings for a future project is not surplus).

The same two outcomes will result when the third step is not conducted. Either way, if you don't plan you will fail.

Lastly, if you have performed your business plan effectively and you still find yourself with insufficient resources there can be only one other reason; that would be a superior or parent department has reduced your resources within the budget period. If this has occurred, the solution is to develop a new business plan.

Challenge:

Diverse customers and expectations

This challenge is also not unique to government however in this instance, government departments are far more impacted, this is because a commercial organization will often have its business structured to provide the right service experience to all of their customer segments. The government agency will often expect the single business unit to service all customers - this is challenging.

So what can you do? In the next chapter you will learn about service reviews. The service review has been around a long time and came into the spotlight a few ago. It has largely gone out of the spotlight because it was perceived to add little value and take too long to perform. I have performed service reviews for many government departments and every single one has brought about positive change. The difference is the objective; many (if not most) reviews have been conducted to meet a regulatory imposed requirement. It is a shame really that more reviewers did not conduct the reviews with a positive outcome as their primary objective as when performed correctly the service review can be a very effective tool.

Challenge:

Red tape

Good old red tape; every business has to deal with some sort of red tape. This is often imposed by governments themselves for a good reason. The red tape can be a challenge for any business to cope with however for a government department it can be suffocating as they are often under stricter scrutiny from fellow government departments. In fact the Australian Federal Government has a target to reduce the impacts of red tape by $1,000,000,000 per year. Unfortunately this is looking like actually adding some red tape due to the approach taken, at least in the short term.

So how do we deal with red tape and avoid the suffocation? With good effective planning. The first step is to determine all of the regulatory and other reporting/red tape requirements.

When you have compiled a complete list of requirements the next step is to plan how you can maintain adherence to the requirements. You should add the resource requirements to your business planning process.

Through monitoring you can be sure you are fulfilling your obligations, both internal and external.

3. Reviewing your services

I briefly discussed the service review in the previous chapter, I will take a little bit more time now and discuss the process in more detail. Firstly I will discuss my experiences with reviewing the services of government departments.

When I first began working as a consultant in the government sector I had not heard a lot about the service review and I instinctively began putting my own approach to it. I immediately began achieving good results, better results than the other consultants with much more government sector experience. I immediately began researching the history and specific intent of the service review and found that it was a regulatory requirement that had come into effect around 15 years earlier. This requirement had since been lifted, however many departments still used it as a means of satisfying reporting requirements. Although it was a regulatory requirement there was no real documented process or robust method, so every practitioner had their own way of going about it; and worse still, some approached it differently each time.

So the first thing I did was to go about developing a framework and documented method with my colleagues. This was completed over the course of a few months while we persevered with the lack of current process and trialed different ideas to prove the future processes. We were following a PDCA cycle in the development of our process. The process, as with every process was never finalized, however we did get a documented process to a high level after much trialing and consultation.

Let's get straight into the steps to reviewing your services. The objective of a service review is to design and develop a service that delivers good value to the community. Value is a term that is used a lot in the lean business process and systems; the process we are following here is very similar to any lean project or review and follows a seven step process.

Steps to reviewing your services:

1) Current State

The first step is to develop a profile of your current state. Without knowing where you currently are it is impossible to make effective change without the help of good luck. Only when you know where you are today can you see where your problems are and what steps are needed to fix the situation.

What services do you deliver?

Make a list of the services you deliver, break it right down to the elements with both internal and external customers. A good tool to use for this is the systems view. The systems view is a tool used to define your customers, processes, suppliers and other interactions. Below is an example of a systems view from a government department I worked with in the past (names & particulars have been changed).

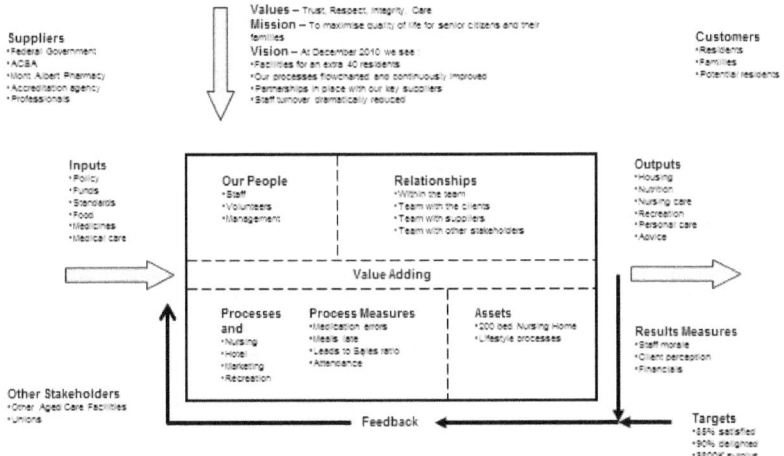

Included in the systems view are your customers, suppliers, inputs, outputs and measurables.

What skills does the team have?

Conduct a skills analysis of the team by having each team member draft a list of their own skills. Each team member should then complete a list of skills held by their peers within the team. The facilitator along with the leadership team then compiles the lists into a complete and accurate skills assessment.

While the team members are doing the above and before the lists are submitted, the Leadership / Management team should develop a list of required skills to perform the tasks and achieve the objectives of the department. At this stage this probably will not be a conclusive list; we will discuss later in this chapter how the skills requirement list will be developed further.

25

The list can be as simple as the below example:

Task / Objective	Skillset Required

Further to the skills analysis, a COWS or SWOT can be conducted. I prefer the use of the COWS method. The COWS analysis is a useful tool that can be used to analyse almost any situation. COWS stands for:

- Challenges: looks at the internal and external factors that may have a negative impact to a successful implementation
- Opportunities: looks at the internal and external factors that may assist in the successful implementation
- Weaknesses: looks at how this change may negatively impact on the business or any business component
- Strengths: looks at how this change will positively impact the business or business component

Unlike the SWOT (strengths, weaknesses, opportunities and threats) analysis, the COWS analysis looks at supporting factors e.g. relationships; before looking at the tangible factors. This provides a more thorough understanding of the current situation and ensures the supporting factors are analysed.

It is often underestimated (until hindsight kicks in) how critical the support of internal and external factors can be on a project. We often discuss, at great length, the project with those that are seen to be directly involved. We need to communicate with the departments and people that may not be directly involved but may be directly or indirectly impacted. This impact could be positive or negative; it doesn't really matter. The fact that communication did not occur will have a negative impact on the project.

The COWS analysis helps us to identify who we need to communicate to as it defines what challenges we are likely to face along the way and also who can be our allies. This is another tool that has been developed from a marketing tool. In many ways managing change in an organization is similar to marketing a product or service. We need to identify what the customer (the business) needs and firstly "sell" the plan to different parts of the business.

A COWS analysis is simply a matrix of four quadrants. These quadrants are labelled Challenges, Opportunities, Weaknesses and Strengths. The below diagram shows an example of a typical COWS analysis.

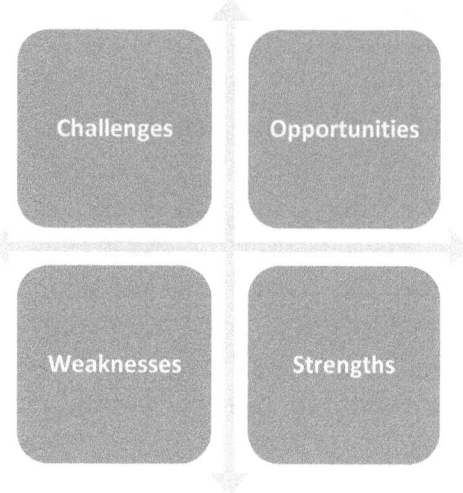

Current KPI's and performance

In the development of your systems view you identified the measurables of the department. Collect data to measure the current status of your service and department. It is good to have internal and external KPI's; internal KPI's measure the team's ability to perform the tasks required and will include financial, OHS and other business measures whereas external KPI's measure the success of the service delivery and the customer satisfaction.

At this stage you are likely to find KPI's that do not add value or tell the real story of your business unit; this will be addressed later in the process. For now, make notes on the validity of your current KPI's so you can reference when the new KPI's are being developed.

2) Consultation

Before we commence with the consultation it is a good practice for the team to define what they believe the customer expectations are. This should be conducted for both internal and external customers. This is done for a couple of reasons, first and foremost as a way to measure how well the team understands their customers.

Consultation within the organization

I always prefer to consult internally within the organization first. Once again this is done for the reason above, and also to understand the internal customers & stakeholders needs and expectations. The internal stakeholders needs are often forgotten about but are an important piece of the puzzle as their needs can be reflective of other external customers needs.

There are two main internal groups to consult with. The first group are internal to the service; this includes team members, team management etc. The second group are external to the service; this can include support services, other parts of the organization delivering different services (depending on your organization type).

The questions you ask in the consultation will differ for both of the above and depending on the type of services you deliver but as a rule, the questions should be framed to achieve qualitative and quantitative responses that provide a measure of your service within your organization. Some of the measures you are looking to understand include:

- Cost to run the service
- Number of clients serviced
- Efficiency and productivity
- Income per employee
- Community significance

Even though you are not running a commercial operation you still to measure against some commercial type metrics. This step in the process should not be rushed and you shouldn't spend too much money on this; don't go into color glossy handouts and external surveys etc. Go and talk to your team members (both internal to the service and external) to talk face to face about what they see and how they measure you.

Consultation with other service providers

The next phase is to consult with other service providers that may provide a similar service to yours. Depending on your particular service this can be reasonably easy or it may be very difficult. There are some service providers that specialize in providing these reports to Government agencies; they will be at a cost, however if you are smart and combine your requirements across the organization it will work out reasonable per department.

If the information is not easily available you may be able to work with a service provider in the local community and build a collaborative working relationship; for this project and for longer term collaboration. What I wouldn't try and do is to attempt to gather the information under the guise of a fake customer or similar. This will only result in distrust. If this fails you can do similar with a service provider from a different locality. This consultation can be challenging, but it is important to have a commercial model to benchmark against.

Consultation with the community / customer

The third phase of consultation is with the customers and broader community. It is necessary to consult with both your customers and the broader communities as these groups are likely to have different expectations for both the type of service provided and the level of service provided.

I always start with the direct customers as this is an easy way to get started. By now, with all of the internal and external consultation you should be experts in developing the questions, identifying the targets and soliciting the responses.

When designing the consultation with direct users of the service, always stay clear from leading questions. You want to know their honest thoughts and experiences. For this reason it is a good idea to have the staff directly involved with them as part of the service delivery involved to reassure but not too directly involved in the consultation that they can intentionally or unintentionally impact the information.

The final consultation is with the broader community and we do this to understand what the broader community expectations from our service are and also to understand how much the community knows about our service. We don't often know just how effective our marketing services are; this is a good chance to find out.

The questions for this exercise will be different to those for your customers as these targets do not currently use the service. You will be asking more questions about whether they know of the service and what their expectations of the service would be. If they are previous users or future users and if they have any knowledge of others using the service or similar services

3) Comparison / Gap Analysis

By this stage you will have a good understanding of your service, business unit and team backed up by data. From your consultation and benchmarking you will also have a picture of what best practice looks like. Best practice is an interesting term that can often hold this process back when it is misunderstood. This is my take on the term:

Best practice is an unattainable future state; so it is a journey to achieve the benchmark status is every element (both tangible and intangible) of your service and business unit operations. As the benchmark keeps moving as new and higher reaching standards are developed, you need to adjust your target. Being at the leading edge of innovation and setting the benchmark keeps you in an exciting position.

In this step you take your current state collected from the previous steps, compare against what you know of best practice and perform a gap analysis.

Current State

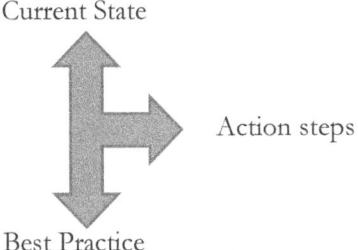

Action steps

Best Practice

To uncomplicate the comparison, it is good to break it down and look at each element rather than in its entirety. So firstly, list out the elements of your service (if you have done this as a spreadsheet earlier you can copy it over) with three additional columns:

- Current state

- Best practice

- Difference

In the second column enter your current state data or status for each element. In the third column enter the best practice that you strive to achieve and finally in the fourth column enter the difference between the two.

Obviously, if the cells contain pure numerical data the calculation to complete the fourth column will be simple, however in the likely event that your cells contain softer or less tangible status or targets you will have to be a little more creative.

The more time you spend on this step to define the gaps between your current state and best practice the easier the next step will be. It's important here for me to add that "best practice" doesn't necessarily need to be your goal for every element of your process. That must seem a bit strange after all of the earlier talk about bench marking and best practice but let me explain why. For an organization to achieve best practice in every way, in every element it will have certain repercussions to the organization; it will likely result in disjointed processes that struggle to interact. What we want is to become a best practice example of an organization / department; meaning holistically we are providing best practice service to the customer / community. There is a difference between the two which should become clearer in the next step.

4) Design the future

This is where you and the team can dream; blue sky thinking is what we are after here. Go through the work element list and for each element talk about what the future could be.

At step 1 we introduced the Systems View concept. You would have noticed the example contained the following items that were not discussed at the time:

- Values

- Vision

- Mission

The first thing you should be doing at step 4 is to develop *agreed* Team and Service Values, Vision and Mission statements. I stress the word agreed here; we need buy-in from the team. If you already have these, then now is the time to review and revise them. You now know what the expectations from the community, customers and organization are for your service, so what better time to develop these statements with that knowledge freshly captured. I like to start off by setting team rules, a team charter which encompasses the rules and a service charter. The Vision, Mission and Values are then quite easy to pull out from that information.

New next step is to revisit your element worksheet and add another column. This column is to record what your future for this element looks like. This is where you dream big; remember, not every detail you enter here will be immediately possible. Some may take months and years to achieve, others will be relatively short term implementations. If your entire plan can be implemented in a few short months then you have probably set the bar too low.

Now you have dreamed big the next thing is to perform a reality check; so you have your long term vision for the service, what can you realistically change in the next 6 months? Which of the elements will give you the biggest gain for the cost and effort required? A simple chart can help you to prioritize the list as in the example below.

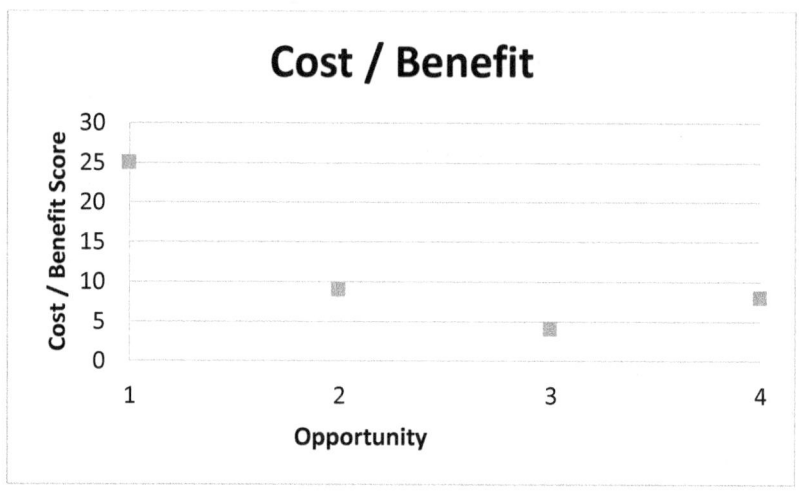

In this chart each opportunity is rated for the cost / effort to implement from 5 to 1 (5 being low cost and low effort, 1 being high cost and high effort). Then rated for the benefit to the customer / service from 1 to 5 (5 being high benefit, 1 being low benefit). It is quite easy to see from the example that option 1 is the most attractive with a combined score of 25. I multiply the two scores together as this creates a greater spread of total scores and an easier to read chart when a high number of options are graphed. From this activity you will have a prioritized list of opportunities that will later be presented as an action plan.

Once this is completed, you then need to conduct a gap analysis on the Skills Matrix now that your future state work elements have been defined. Follow the steps outlined earlier in this chapter to complete your updated Skills Matrix and conduct a gap analysis. The result from this will be a skills analysis and Training Plan.

Skills Matrix Example:

Element	Skill	Joe	Barry	Kim	Jerry
Customer Service	Problem solving	4	2	1	4
Customer Service	Needs analysis	1	3	3	2

As part of this step you should develop new KPI's for the team and individual tasks. This is not the place for individual KPI's for the team, the individual work plan is the process for the team members. What we are looking at here is the process and team KPI's. Big data is one of the new business buzz words, for me it has its place however you need to be mindful of drowning in data if too much data is collected without resources to mine and utilize.

When setting KPI's there are a couple of important guidelines to remember and take note of for best results and value.

1. Only measure what matters:

If you cannot or do not make a decision based on what the measurement tells you, why are you measuring it?

2. Measure what you need to know:

Conversely, if there is a question that often comes up, develop a KPI to provide you with the information when you need it.

3. SMART

Specific

Measurable

Achievable

Relevant

Time-bound

Follow these three guidelines and you will have a good balance between enough detailed data and drowning in numbers.

I like to create a future state process map or value stream map (VSM). The VSM will be discussed in a later chapter. I do this to show the improvements visually both to the team and the larger organization. A major part of any improvement process is the engagement of the team/s. By presenting the process in a few different formats i.e. systems view, process map, spreadsheets you are catering to different peoples learning styles and comforts.

5) Put the plan into place

What good is all of this work if no action takes place? Worse than no work at all. Really, you are better off doing none of the above steps if you do not follow through with action.

The first step in this section is to develop a clear concise action plan. The action plan needs to include:

- The actions to be taken. It is easy to document the problem here instead so be sure you have the solution or action.

- The person who is responsible for the completion of the action. This person can delegate the action but it's important to keep the person *responsible* for the completion here.

- Completion due date

- Action status. I include this to ensure the document remains "live" and is in use rather than forgotten.

- Roadblocks or bottlenecks encountered.

- A column to record comments.

A simple spreadsheet will do the job. There are software packages you can purchase to capture this but in my opinion and experience a simple spreadsheet is easier to set up and maintain and gives you the capability to report on progress.

The next step is the most important of all; we need to take action. If action is not taken, all of the hard work of the preceding steps will be a total waste.

6) Review, review, review

Now the tasks have commenced and the action plan is in the process of being implemented it is critical to review the progress to plan as a team regularly. It would be great if this wasn't required and every project team could depend on every task being completed on time without issue, but in the reality every person on the team usually has other tasks that may become priority as well as other competing pressures. These combined with other road blocks that may arise mean it is absolutely necessary to come together regularly to maintain focus and assist with problem solving.

The frequency of meetings will be dependent on a number of things:

- Maturity of the team. Is the team experienced in working together?

- Experience level of the individuals.

- The maturity of the organization. Are there known constraints within the organization that may lead to road blocks.

Generally I like to hold the meetings fortnightly as a base and adjust the timing based on answers to the above questions. It is a good practice to rotate the chairing of the meeting to share the responsibility and spread the ownership of the project.

Each person with responsibility should report on the following as a minimum:

- Progress to plan / status

- Struggles / roadblocks encountered and how these have been managed

- Constraints requiring assistance

- Expected completion if different from target completion date

Keep the review meetings short and directly to the point; a stand-up meeting can keep things moving. Never bring food or snacks for the team as we are trying to bring a culture of productivity and efficiency to the team.

7) Start over

So at what frequency should you conduct this level of service review? The Executive should team should develop a schedule for each service unit to be reviewed over a three year period. This provides sufficient gap between the repeated audits of each unit while also pushing the organization to work through the schedule. Conversely, don't over review the individual business units; I find every three years is a good base. If you have a "problem child" that is coming from a very low base you may want to increase the frequency to two years.

The most critical instruction: let each team complete their review. Don't pull the team apart during the review or change the service dramatically during the review. Leave it alone until the review is complete; it can be tempting to make changes to the service during the review as you find some low hanging fruit but to follow this temptation before the team is ready to implement is a mistake and often results in the review not finding a completion stage.

4. 5S

Apart from the service review, the most effective change you can drive through your services is the introduction and effective implementation of 5S. The following 5S implementation plan provides an effective roadmap to introducing 5S into any organization.

There are a few prerequisites that need to be in place and followed. Without some of these prerequisites success will be difficult at best, without others, success is still very achievable; I think you will be able to identify which are the most important.

Buy-in

This may seem obvious however it requires discussion. It is critical that you have the buy-in from two different groups within your business.

The first group is the executive management. You will need to have the buy-in and support of this group to firstly drive the changes at their level, without this buy-in it is highly likely that you will spend a large portion of your time justifying your program. You will also need their commitment to gain approval for any capital and/or overhead expenses.

The second group you will need the buy-in from is from the target work area. This can be any part of the organization – 5S works just as effectively in the office as it does in the workshop; whatever the work area, you will need to have the buy-in from the team.

Buy-in or ownership is critically important in any change program. It will make or break your success in implementing a sustainable 5S culture. You can achieve some small and not so small improvements without full buy-in however, you will struggle to achieve the great successes you can with it.

Defined Area

As I said above, the selected area can be from anywhere in the business. Saying this, I have always found it best if the initial test area is within the workshop or similar environment. Depending on your organization these areas will be where your business performs the most "real work" and you will find the biggest visual improvements – make a good improvement here and you will likely gain positive exposure for the team and the 5S project (this can be very important early in the lean journey). The important thing at this point is that the area chosen is quite small and contained. Whether this is the first time a 5S program has been run in the organization or this is the final area to undertake the change, it is a good idea to limit the size of the area in the program. There is no limit to the number of target 5S areas you can have in the organization, actually it is almost a case of the more the better.

So, we have chosen a small work area, what's next?

Defined Teams

When you get into the work area, you'll need small teams to work together during various stages of the process. These teams should include at least one person NOT from the working area whenever possible. The reason for this is to bring 'fresh eyes' to the team. A fresh set of eyes will often 'see' opportunities that are missed by those working within the area as it is natural to become blind to "normality".

Selection of the teams is an important step and should be done to enable the teams to achieve the best outcomes possible. Each team needs to have a leader – even if you choose to not designate a leader, a natural leader needs to be present to maintain the focus.

You may identify people in your group that are not 'team players' – these people need to be placed in teams that have the capacity to drive effectiveness from every team member and a strong leader or leadership group to ensure this team member is kept in line. Don't give these people an easy ride they need to go into a team that will manage this well – you may find this team needs to be led by a supervisor or manager; maybe even yourself.

Make sure the teams have clearly defined targets and areas of responsibility. Remember, what gets measured, gets managed!

Budget and Authority

It may be difficult for your first program, but a small budget will make the process more streamlined and will help achieve greater early success. There will be small items that need to be purchased during the first two stages; if you are able to purchase these without waiting for approval you will not only have faster success, but it will also help with buy-in from the team.

You need to ensure you have some authority from the organization to make relevant decisions during the program. Most of these decisions will be small and will have little or no impact on the running of the organization.

Current State Photographs

Before you begin making any changes it is a very good idea to take photographs of the current situation. It is very easy to forget where you have come from once the changes have been made. They say a picture paints a thousand words – well that is only true if it is the right picture. So how do you take the right picture?

- Find a good vantage point to get the best perspective for your photograph

- Mark or identify the spot the photograph is taken from

- Take before and after photographs from the same location to increase the visual impact your photographs make

- Take as many photographs as you can at both the before and after stage. With digital cameras you can afford to take plenty and discard those that are not suitable for use.

Now to the 5S process.

Step One - Sort

Aim:

The aim of this step is to remove anything from the area that should not be there. The first thing we need to do here is to define "what shouldn't be in the area".

A good way to define this is:

Usage / Value	Disposition
Junk , no value	Rubbish
Excess consumables	Return to store
Not needed	Red Tag area
Daily usage	Visible and accessible
Weekly usage	Store in work area
Monthly usage	Store centrally / return to stores
Less than monthly	Return to stores or store outside work area

This is a guide only and it should be tailored to your work environment and infrastructure. It does provide a starting point though. With these guidelines in place let's get started with sorting.

What you'll need:

- A 5S Red Tag area (this area will be discussed shortly).
- Red Tags (optional) - these are available online or you can make your own.

- Good understanding of tool requirements to undertake the work in the area.
- Red Tag register (optional) – used to record all items removed to the red tag area and later removed from the area. This can be handy in case someone asks for something at a later date.
- Blank 5S requirement work sheet (optional).

How:

Now the fun begins, start working through the area in teams of two or three people – as defined earlier. Remember in this step all you are doing is sorting what should and shouldn't be in the area. Each team should be armed with red tags and a red tag register.

As an item is identified as not being required for use in the area, attached a red tag and populate the red tag register. The red tags should be numbered to enable easier identification later.

Remove the item to the designated red tag area. All of these items will be analyzed closely later.

Be brutal! Everything in doubt should be removed to the red tag area during this phase. Have the discussion later.

This should be one of the fastest phases of the entire program. If you find your team is taking too long to discuss items as they go, you should intervene. Any discussion should be held during the next phase of the sorting step.

Ask this question "When will this item be used?" If the answer is unknown or is greater than a week then remove it from the area and attach a red tag. If the answer cannot be agreed upon or takes an unreasonable amount of time to answer then remove it from the area, relocate it to the red tag area and attach a red tag.

After sorting through the area you will have only the tools required to do the job at hand in the area and a red tag area with a large number of tagged items. If the quantity of items in the red tag area is small then either you were not brutal enough or your area was reasonably well kept beforehand.

The red tag area needs to be in a position that can be left for at least a couple of days without creating any issues. If you can arrange for racks in the area this will help to better organize things. The red tag area needs to be clearly defined and identified and should be partitioned off from the work areas.

Now you have to hold off on doing anything. Let the work in the area carry on as usual for two to three days. This will either a) reinforce that the removed items are not required in the work area or b) force the retrieval of some of the items from the red tag area. It really doesn't matter which of these two occur as this is just confirming the sort.

Do not discourage the retrieval of items as long as they are used for their designed purpose. What does this mean exactly? If they retrieve a screwdriver to scrape paint for example then this should not be retrieved as it not being used for the designed purpose. In this instance, a paint scraper will be added to the 5S requirements work sheet and later purchased once approved.

The next action is to conduct an auction for the items in the red tag area. Many practitioners conduct the auction shortly after removing the items, in my experience this will result in many of the unnecessary items being 'bought' back by the users. By taking two to three days to a week before conducting the auction, the users will now be used to operating without the items.

The auction should take place within the red tag area and should be conducted by the area team leader, supervisor or manager to make it more interesting.

- Each item is raised for the auction in turn
- Rather than auctioning for a price, a bidder need only raise their hand to 'purchase' the item
- The only rule here is they must have a better than good reason for needing the item

When an item is returned to the work area, monitor the use of the item over a period of time to ensure the excess tools do not begin to build up again. This sorting process can be performed at a regular interval – annually is a good start. Any more than this and you will be over analyzing and less frequent and you could come back to quite a big task again.

All items in the red tag area need to have a disposition. Whether the item is returned to the work area, is moved into storage/warehouse, is relocated to another work area or is scrapped, every item must be dealt with.

After the initial sort, you shouldn't need to have a great deal of input into future sort exercises. It is important with any of the lean tools (as with other business tools) that the tools become ingrained into the day to day operations of the business – this means every employee has a responsibility to incorporate the tools into their daily work. Small actions repeated and built upon over a period of time make a big impact.

Sort Guidelines

- Every item in the area needs to be assessed for requirement and usage frequency
- Set up your red tag area
- Remove all unused items to the red tag area
- Wait
- Hold your auction
- Make sure a solid argument exists for the return of any items

Step 2 – Set in Order

Aim:

The aim of this step is to ensure every item needed in the area has a home – A place for everything and everything in its place.

What you'll need:

- The completed 5S requirements work sheet
- Current 5S Audit results

How:

Setting in order should be started soon after the sort has been completed and the red tag auction is complete. The longer the wait between steps, the more likely you will need to sort again before applying the set in order phase. Basically, this is about making the items easily accessible every time to improve efficiency and reduce quality issues and costs (through replacements and efficiency). What does setting in order apply to? In short, it applies to everything:

- OHS information and equipment
- Tools
- Inventory items
    - Raw materials – in an office this could be inputs to your business process
    - Sub-assemblies
    - Consumables
- Work instructions
- Work schedules
- Samples
- Quality inspection equipment and information
- Reporting documents and tools
- Contact details and systems for supervisors

If you have a floor plan on CAD it will make your life easier, otherwise you will need to sketch out the work space. Earlier I mentioned the good practice of working in a small area for each project; this is when you will understand why it is good practice. There are a couple of reasons for this:

- A smaller area can be set in order in a shorter amount of time
- The cost to complete the set in order of a smaller area is far less than that of a larger work area. This cost takes into account both material and labor
- The benefits will be realized sooner, this will help with momentum for the next areas and also help with buy-in from all parties. Once management sees the results that can be achieved through the sorting and setting in order of a small area, they will be more supportive of future projects.

Back to sketching the work area, if you have a CAD diagram of the work area even better, but there is nothing wrong with sketching. A pencil sketch will be ok to get you started, but it is a good idea to follow this up with a drawing at least close to scale. This drawing is of the current state and should show as near everything as possible. Before you start to amend the layout, take a couple of copies of the raw sketch – this will save you time later when you want to make revisions.

Next you will need the completed 5S requirements sheet and a full list of all of the items used in the area. This list needs to include:

- Raw materials
- Components
- Tools
- Equipment
- Work area
- Inspection equipment

- Inspection work area
- Housekeeping equipment

Before moving on I am going to digress a little and discuss the Plan Do Check Act (PDCA) cycle. Although the PDCA cycle is often referred to as a quality tool, it has a big part to play lean systems also and is very useful in the set in order stage.

Let's go through the PDCA cycle one step at a time.

The process always begins with planning. This step usually takes up to 2/3 of the project timing.

Plan – Analyze what has gone wrong? Find a gap and make a plan to implement countermeasures.

Do – Trial the countermeasure.

Check – Measure the outcomes from the trial to determine the effectiveness.

Act – If the countermeasures provide the desired outcomes – implement on a larger scale and share the lessons learnt. Otherwise develop new countermeasures and return to "Do".

Now we all understand the PDCA cycle, we have to begin the planning of how we will set in order. Just as items that are used frequently are kept within the area, items with the highest frequency usage should be located nearest the user. Further to this there are some good guidelines on workspace ergonomics that can be easily found on the internet; incorporating better Occupational Health & Safety into the layout is a must have. As a general rule, try to limit the amount of movement (particularly twisting and reaching) of the person to reduce the risk of injury and to also improve efficiency.

You will need to draw a revised or future layout for the overall area. This will look at thoroughfares, work flow, material flow and bulk storage options. You are likely to need a number of versions of the future layout, these should not be undertaken by a single person, but should be completed with the input of the entire team. Once you have a number of options drafted, it is time to gain consensus for a single option; a combination of different options can come together to provide a new alternative.

The next step is to draft up the macro work stations within the work area. Hopefully you have taken heed and are working on a relatively small area. You will need to follow the same process as you did with the work area; drafting a few versions and gaining consensus etc.

These two future maps must incorporate storage for every item you listed on both the 5S requirements sheet and the list of items used in the area. Once you have the two plans drafted you will need to put together an action plan of every item and the step by step program of how they will be implemented. One of the first action items should be to apply a cost to the changes and build a business case to gain approval for the capital expenditure. Even if the costs are negligible or your business does not require you to go to this extent, I would implore you to undertake this activity and report the costs and the benefits to your superiors. By doing so, you are showing your own commitment and belief in the 5S process; this should build more buy in from the entire business.

To gain approval for your implementation you will need to show a return on the investment (ROI). This is another reason why you should start with a smaller work area – to keep the capital expenditure down. One of the first and best things I was taught from Toyota training is that some of the best ideas are often not expensive or are even free to implement (excluding of labor costs). Don't dismiss an idea just because it doesn't cost a lot to implement, at the same time you shouldn't dismiss an idea just because it costs some amount for implementation. It all comes down to ROI. To calculate the ROI, it is a simple process of first understanding your costs, then translating these costs into time. Next calculate the savings the changes can bring to the process and then translate these savings into time.

For example:

If the cost of the changes is $15,000 and the savings are $1,000 per week then your ROI is 15 weeks. If the cost is $50,000 and the savings are $800 per week then the ROI is 63 weeks.

As a general rule of thumb, if you have a project with an ROI of less than one year then you should really try and implement it.

Another good way to measure ideas is by using the cost benefit matrix / chart discussed in an earlier chapter.

Once you have the above analysis you can go about gaining approval for financial support. While you are going through the above it is a good idea to "Do" some of the items in a trial. If you wait until financial approval you will lose too much time and also run the risk of requesting capital that is not required while also missing other capital items as the requirements change through the trialing stage. This is the "Do" step in the PDCA cycle and is a critical step in achieving success. Some items cannot be trialed until the approval is gained due to machinery or tooling requirements, however there are usually many that can be trialed.

This will enable you to fine tune the concepts before final implementation. This fine tuning step is the "Check" step in the PDCA cycle; and is where many projects fail. Anyone can have an idea and go and put the idea into practice, however to turn an idea into a sustainable improvement you need to "check" that it is working as planned and that it is realizing the planned (or desired) benefits. The checking stage needs to be structured to ensure what you measure can be used for deeper analysis. In a similar method to a scientific experiment, you need to set the scope of the trial, closely measure and accurately record the outcomes. In reality, the "Do" and "Check" steps are performed simultaneously.

By following these steps you can then "Act" by implementing the final process and layout without excessive modification or difficulty. Some of the main points are below:

- Get the entire team involved in development of the layout and process
- Get buy-in from the business early in the project
- Follow the PDCA cycle to give your project the best chance of success
- Work on a small area at a time
- Complete the Set In Order for each small area before moving onto the next area
- Every item (tools, inventory, inspection etc) must have a home once this step is complete

Step 3 – Shine

Aim:

The aim of this step is to clean the surfaces, equipment and tools to enable fast identification of a problem.

What you'll need:

- Cleaning equipment

- Tooling / plant operating and maintenance instructions

How:

This could be a small chapter! What we are doing is cleaning, but it really is a lot more than just cleaning. Like every other activity there needs to be plan, and the plan is structured around the PDCA cycle.

Question:

What are you going to clean?

Answer:

In short, everything in the area. To really understand the answer to this question we must explore another question. We can then return to this answer.

Question:

Why are we cleaning?

Answer:

There can be many reasons we should perform the cleaning step in the 5S program. The first is to ensure we are starting our journey from the best position. If we ignore this step then we will never really see the work area as good as it could be. Therefore we will be starting off from a poor position and will never reach our ultimate goal. If we follow the Shine step, we will set a high standard, this will be discussed more in the next chapter – Step 5 Standardize.

Another, and the main reason for following this step is to provide the best operating environment for machinery, plant and people. Only with this environment in place will you be in a position to identify an issue with the equipment early enough to rectify the problem before it becomes critical. If this environment is not in place it is quite likely the first you know of a problem is when it is too late – either a defect has been passed on to the customer or the equipment has broken down and has caused unplanned downtime.

Now back to the first question; the short answer was we clean everything. In reality we need to clean more than everything. Impossible I know, but it needs to be made clear just how far the cleaning needs to go. Clean everything you think needs cleaning, and then look further for more cleaning opportunities.

Start by cleaning the general floor area, sweeping the floor, then follow with a commercial cleaning system if possible. Next you should clean all machinery, tables, benches and racking. Every surface area needs to be cleaned at this initial stage. The machinery needs to be treated even further.

- All guarding is removed and cleaned
- All oil marks and leaks are cleaned
- All leaks need to be repaired where practical
- Under machines should be cleaned

In an office environment this can be modified to removing all computers, phones, printers etc. from the desks and floor area.

This may seem like a lot of effort for not a lot of gain, but it is very important this step is followed as you will soon realize the benefits of the initial clean. This will positively impact:

- Team morale
- Product quality
- Operating efficiency
- DIFOT (Delivery In Full On Time)
- Customer satisfaction
- Resource efficiency

The Big Clean:

Every one has had some exposure to cleaning I'm sure, some much more than others – depending on how we grew up I guess, so there shouldn't be a great need for too much instruction, however I will say the best method I have found is to divide and conquer.

Divide the work area into smaller areas on the layout and assign a responsible person or team (teams will be more effective) to clean each of these smaller areas. After the clean, inspection of the areas needs to be performed; this can be by the facilitator, a manager / supervisor or by cross checking by the cleaning team. The latter can be very effective when the teams are competitive and have bought into the process. Only when the cleaning is complete has the Shine step been completed – remember to set expectations prior to the commencement.

After all the cleaning is complete and the inspectors are satisfied it is time for a team walk to verify the standards have been met. Get the entire team together and walk slowly through the work area. The facilitator or manager need to be the 'guide' through the walk. Be very critical (but practical) through this step, this is a chance for the expectations to be set, reinforced and understood.

Once there is full agreement that the shine is at acceptable levels you can move onto the next step.

Step 4 – Standardize

Aim:

The purpose of this step is to make the work practices and flow consistent from station to station. Any sufficiently skilled person should be able to work at any work station and locate the tools and parts to do the job.

How:

This step is the one that causes the most backward sliding in organizations. The first two or three steps are quite active and therefore rewards are realized quickly. This step is less activity based.

There are a couple of distinct ways to look at the standardizing step. The first looks at turning the new work area into the "standard" – in effect following the ISO 9001 rule of clearly defining standards to be achieved. The second is to standardize the work stations throughout the work-centre and greater business – this will enable any person from any area to more easily work in a different work area.

Let's begin by looking at the first definition. Hopefully you followed the instructions in Step One and have taken some "Before" photographs. Now is when you can use them. Print out some good (bad) examples of how the work area was before the first 3S's. Take these printouts to the work area and take some new photographs to show the changes and new work area after the work has been performed. It is important now to take the after photographs from the same aspect and angle as the before photographs. It is a good idea to create a map early on and mark where the before shots were taken.

Once the photographs have been taken successfully, we can build a 5S storyboard. A magnetic whiteboard will be ideal for this purpose. If you have an 1800x1200mm whiteboard you can use half for the storyboard. A photograph of the team can be placed on the top of the storyboard next to the title. This should include all members of the team that work in the area and who were involved in the project. If you had a person who was uncooperative and was not involved in the project they can be left out of the photograph. Conversely if you had a person who was uncooperative but was involved reluctantly, this person should be included in the photograph.

What you'll need to create the storyboard:

- 1800x1200mm magnetic whiteboard
- Before photographs
- After photographs
- Team photograph
- Permanent markers or whiteboard tape
- Lamination pouches
- Magnetic clips or magnets
- Headings / notes etc – laminated
- Large colored arrows - laminated

Divide the board in half with the permanent marker or whiteboard tape (the other half will be used in the next chapter). You can layout your storyboard however you prefer, the following is how mine are laid out – I always try to keep them to a standardized layout.

- Position your main header centered at the top
- Place your team photo to the left of the heading
- Position all of your "before" photo's on the left
- Position arrows to the right of the before photo's
- Position "after" photo's to the right of the arrows
- Position any notes or descriptions directly to the right of the photographs

Some things to keep in mind:

- Less is often more
  o Try not to clutter the board
- Make sure the layout "tells a story" and isn't just pictures on a board

- Make the photo's as large as practical to enable easy viewing

It's quite important that the board is actually handed over to the 5S team at this time. This is why the team photograph is added to the board – to promote ownership and responsibility. Even without going to the next level this storyboard should provide some level of responsibility to maintain the new current state.

The "after" images will set in stone the new minimum standard for housekeeping in this area. At this point you should bring other team leaders, supervisors and managers through the area to showcase the work that has been undertaken. Have the team members talk about the changes and tell the story through the storyboard. This will further promote ownership and increase pride in the area. Promote the area through tool-box meetings, management meetings etc. to heighten the profile throughout the business.

Celebrate with the team! I know we are now only 4/5ths through the process, but the 5th step is very much driven by the facilitator or manager and not the team. So now is the time to celebrate; it can be small or big – depending on the project itself. Whatever you choose, you need to celebrate; this is an absolute must in every change project and is a pivotal step in any change management system.

Now to the second definition: to standardize the work stations and work areas throughout the work centre and greater business. This definition will bring far greater gains than the first definition however will also be a longer and more involved process requiring great commitment. The benefits you will realize by following this step can turn your business into a world class performer! Yes it really is that powerful. And the best news is that the hard work has already been done. By creating a benchmark area in your business you have proven that 5S works, is achievable and provides tangible benefits to the organization.

The first thing you want to do is standardize the workstations within the work area. Once again, earlier I said to make sure the initial trial area was small, well now you can expand on that and spread the 5S word. Only now you and your team have the added benefit of what you have already learned through your initial trial area.

Depending on your workplace, this may be as simple as copying the work you have already done in the trial area. However it may be necessary and it is highly advisable to follow all of the steps again. By doing this you will ensure the best results and eliminate complacency. Remember, to become a lean organization takes planning and effort – there are no shortcuts.

Once you have worked your way through the work area, you should further standardize throughout the rest of the business. Obviously, the further you move away from the initial trial area, the more important it becomes to closely follow the preceding steps. This process can be just as effective in a workshop environment or an office environment.

Upon the completion of this step you should have a business that is operating with a high level of 5S. This will create a strong foundation for further continuous improvement initiatives.

Before moving on to the next step, I think it is important to briefly discuss the meaning of "standardized". It can be easy to become too focused on standardizing to make all work centre's very similar. While this may be close to the true definition of the word; in the context of lean systems and quality management this will hinder your progress. In the context we require; by standardizing we are copying the process and resultant best practice work area. In essence we are following a standardized process to achieve an outcome which is to a required standard or level to enable the required tasks to be performed in the most efficient and effective manner.

Step 5 Sustain

Aim:

The aim of this step should be quite clear from the title: to sustain the progress made through the 5S program.

How:

The implementation of a sustainable 5S system is the obvious desired outcome from a 5S program. Unfortunately, as mentioned earlier in this book, most businesses embarking on the journey never achieve it. Most will work through to setting in order (and do this step quite well) before losing momentum. This then becomes a sort, set in order, begin shine, other priorities, sort ... you get the idea. You need to make sure this does not become you.

Ideally you will follow this step with standardizing across the business as discussed in the previous chapter.

According to dictionary.com sustain means "to keep up or keep going, as an action or process". So it is pretty obvious that by sustaining our 5S program we are looking to ensure it keeps going. Sounds easy right? Well it can be, if done right.

There are really two ways to sustain any business process both are easy in different ways and both are difficult in different ways.

Manually

This method works by management enforcing the continual maintenance of the new system. This can be achieved with a few methods:

- Linking all system requirements to position descriptions
- Involve management in layered audits
- Linking audit results to position description and or bonus schemes
- Layered reporting of audit results and program outcomes

The list here could be very long but I think you should get the drift from this list. All of these methods will work to some extent by themselves, however to get the best results you can combine more than one or even all of them.

Pros

Some of the pros of using this type of system to sustain your 5S program are:

- Management involvement
    o Through layered audits, management will be forced to "walk the Gemba" – place of value adding. Walking the Gemba can also be known as Genchi Genbutsu – "Go and see"
- High accountability from team members
- Hierarchal ownership of the new system
- While the accountability is measured, the system is highly likely to be upheld

Cons

Some of the cons of using this type of system are:

- Reliance on enforcement for system success
- Lack of true ownership by the team
- Lack of drive from the team members can result in ad hoc system compliance
    o System may appear sustained during times of review or audits, however in normal practice may be non compliant
    o This is due to "enforced compliance" by management. This can be more of an issue when weak bonus schemes are applied

Auto / Embedded

This method relies on strong change management skills by the facilitator / leadership team to create a powerful sense of ownership within the team. This can be achieved by using some of the following techniques:

- Continuous communication between management and the team
  - o Communication must be open, honest and cyclical
- Team involvement throughout the program
  - o This has been discussed in earlier chapters, however cannot be underestimated
- Management involvement in activities
  - o Management involvement can help create greater connection, trust and communication between management and team members

Pros

Some of the pros of using this system are:

- True ownership by the team
- Team driven improvements
- Low reliance on management to drive further improvements
- Empowerment of workforce
- Better integration between workforce and management
  - o This can have a long term positive impact on organizational culture
  - o Reduce potential for labor disputes
- System involvement is managed by team members

Cons

Some of the cons of using this system are:

- Potential for reduced management involvement post activities
  - This can reduce some of the positives from above
- It is possible for some teams to lose direction without involvement from managers
  - Some team members just will not accept empowerment or ownership of a process

From this list of pros and cons the only certainty is they are both viable options – both bring very different benefits to the process. These benefits cannot be underestimated. How you go about this step of your 5S program will have the greatest impact on future improvement projects in the organization. If this step is implemented in a structured and measured way your chances of success will be greatly improved.

Just as in every previous step, by following the PDCA cycle through this stage you will follow a structured, focused and planned method to achieving sustainability. I would recommend using a combination of both options to achieve the best result with maximum benefits.

Sustaining your program does not start at this step; in reality it starts way back at the beginning. By achieving good buy-in from all stake holders from the outset, you can now call up that ownership from management and team members alike. If you were able to achieve good buy-in this step will not be at all difficult – however, if you received only superficial buy-in then you could be in for a challenge. Early planning (with the PDCA cycle) will also make this task easier.

So how are we going to sustain your 5S program? There are a few steps that can be taken to ensure sustainability.

1. Develop a 5S audit sheet
    1.1. Templates can be downloaded from many websites for free. Visit www.mlbc.com.au to download one example.
    1.2. Conduct audits daily by the team members initially. This can later be reduced to weekly once the system is well sustained
        1.2.1. Make every team member responsible for something on the audit sheet
    1.3. Display the audit sheet on the 5S storyboard
        1.3.1. This is where you can use the spare half of the board discussed earlier
    1.4. Graph the weekly results on a web diagram
    1.5. Record the results in a spreadsheet – these results can be graphed to show improvements or declines over time with trends
2. Run a layered audit program
    2.1. Begin with the team leaders and supervisors conducting a weekly audit
    2.2. Management, Quality & HR should perform a monthly audit
        2.2.1. This can be rotated through the different managers
    2.3. A quarterly audit should be performed by executive management
        2.3.1. Once again, this can be on a rotational schedule

3. Results from all audits should be displayed on the 5S Storyboard alongside graphs showing trends
4. Results also should be reported and discussed as part of any management reporting system
5. Site visitors should be sought after – show off the work you have done
6. Encourage other departments to implement their own 5S program
    6.1. Run competitions between departments to drive further improvements and instill a sense of pride in the teams.
7. Push – keep driving the 5S culture throughout the organization
    7.1. There will be times when you feel like you are the only one pushing, but it is critical for the program success that you maintain the push

Remember, this will not happen by itself, anything worthwhile needs commitment and persistence.

5. Value Stream Mapping

Value stream mapping (VSM) is a tool that I have used successfully in many organizations in many industries including Local Government. When I first went to apply my trade in Local Government I was challenged as to how effective I and the tools would be in that environment. My approach to this was to take on the challenge; give me the (anecdotally) worst performing unit in the organization and I'll use the tools to turn it around.

The area in question was the Town Planning Department. The department was missing its statutory requirements by a whopping 200% and was regularly one of the lowest performing across the entire state! I decided to use two specific tools in this project; VSM and 5S. These were followed and accompanied by Kaizen and Standardized Work. There were a number of other tools used throughout the project, however VSM and 5S had both the greatest impacts and the majority of time / training.

This particular project lasted six months not including follow-up project reviews. The results from the project were very exciting, with a 92% efficiency improvement achieved at the 3 month stage, further improving to over 100% by the 6 month project close. I share this story to show this really does work; VSM is the most powerful tool in the Lean Toolkit for analyzing a business, team and processes.

The key to using VSM in a government organization is changing the mindset and seeing the processes as Value Streams. We are delivering value to the community; we are not a charity not for profit. No matter what department of an organization you are in, you are delivering value. Remember this, if nothing else from this book remains with you, this is the key. This will be discussed in further detail in Chapter 7.

Back to the VSM; so how do you start the process of creating a VSM? Well firstly let's discuss when to create a VSM. There are two distinct times to create a VSM:

1) To capture the current state of a process before business improvement activities commence

2) To design and model the future state processes during the improvement process

The following pages provide a step by step guide to developing your VSM

Scope the VSM

Before you start on developing a VSM you have to scope the work. Are you going to map the entire business unit or a specific process within the unit? If you have a specific process within the unit that is obviously an issue then it is fine to start with this process. However, when you are using the VSM to support your Service Review the entire business unit must be mapped. Let's take a look at the term Value Stream Map:

- Value: relative worth, merit, or importance

- Stream: a continuous flow or succession of anything

- Map: a maplike delineation, representation or reflection of anything

So a Value Stream Map is a representation of flow of relative worth or importance in the view of the customer. What does the customer see as value and how do you deliver it? It's that simple.

After scoping the VSM, the next thing to do is find a space to display the map. This is often called a war room and needs to have sufficient wall space or windows to display the entire map and workings. If you do not have this space availability it's ok, a series of flip charts can work almost as well. It just means the map will be displayed by turning the pages rather than from left to right.

Once we have these precursor activities out of the way we can start looking at capturing the process.

Process Map

No matter how well you believe you know and understand the process, this needs to be the first step. There are a few reasons for this:

- Clarity of the process. Even when you really know the process there is something about seeing it on paper that helps you see it differently and more clearly.

- Help others see the process. Even if you do accurately understand the process it is likely others in the team do not have the same level of understanding and a process map provides a simple view of the process.

- Agreement and consensus. It is important for the team to agree on the current state process before going to the next step. There may be variations as different people really do perform things differently, especially in the current state, however these differences need to be documented and understood now otherwise disagreement will come up later in the process.

There are a couple of options when developing the process map. Each of the options can be effective and it really comes down to which you prefer and are more comfortable with. The only rule is really to ensure the team creates the process map and not any individual.

Option 1 – Start at the start

As the name suggests with this option you are going to start documenting from the beginning process. I like to list the main inputs at the very beginning or at the very least where the inputs come from (suppliers – can be internal).

Add the forward (customer or downstream) processes to the map with connectors to indicate the direction of flow. After the third option below I will show an example with the main elements and formats.

One of the challenges of using this option is what to do when the process splits to more than a single path. This can be managed by either showing all pathways on the same map or alternatively, move some off-page to another sub-process map.

Option 2 – Start at the end

This is my preferred method and as the name suggests you start at the end process. In contrast to the first option I will write down the outputs and customers at the bottom of the board (I generally perform the draft on the white board before transcribing to either paper or software) before recording the final step in the process.

The main benefit to using this option is that it is often easier to accurately determine the input step to a process than it is to determine the output steps. I do this by asking the simple question "how did you get to this step?". The answer to this question is usually the preceding step.

The challenge to this option is, it may take some time for the team to understand why we are starting at the end. The team (or some participants at least) may have a mental block to accepting this method, however when the team opens its minds the information will start to flow.

Option 3 – Start at a midpoint

With this option you start anywhere in the process and work forwards and backwards from the start point. This option is good for inexperienced groups as it is less rigid in its approach and does allow more freedom.

The main challenge with this approach is it can become confusing and messy as a result of the added freedom.

My favorite approach is option 2 – starting at the end so I will use this approach in the following example. I will map a common process in many government organizations, the Local Town Planning Application approval process.

I like to use Microsoft Visio for documenting my process maps as it is intuitive and simple to use. Before I start on the process map there is one other thing that needs to be discussed. That is the difference between a standard and a deployment chart. A deployment or cross functional chart is divided into operational groups or departments. I use the deployment chart whenever practical to provide an easy visual way of defining responsibilities within the process.

We will start with the scope of the process map:

This will be a high level (low detail) map capturing only internal process steps managed within the department. Excluded will be any external process step (Council approval, planning and other consultants, community consultation, building surveyors etc).

As my preferred method is to start at the end I'll follow this methodology. As we are looking at a high level map with only internal elements the last action with the Planning team will be in the administration team preparing the report for Council. Moving backwards from there, the input is the approved report from the Manager.

The Manager receives the report from the Planner and there is likely to be some rework cycle in here depending on the experience level and capability of the Planner.

The Planner completes their report with information provided by the customer and this step may also require a rework loop as the customer is likely to be guided by the Planner regarding the level of information required. Each job is assigned to the Planners by the Manager from the information collated by the Administration team from the customer.

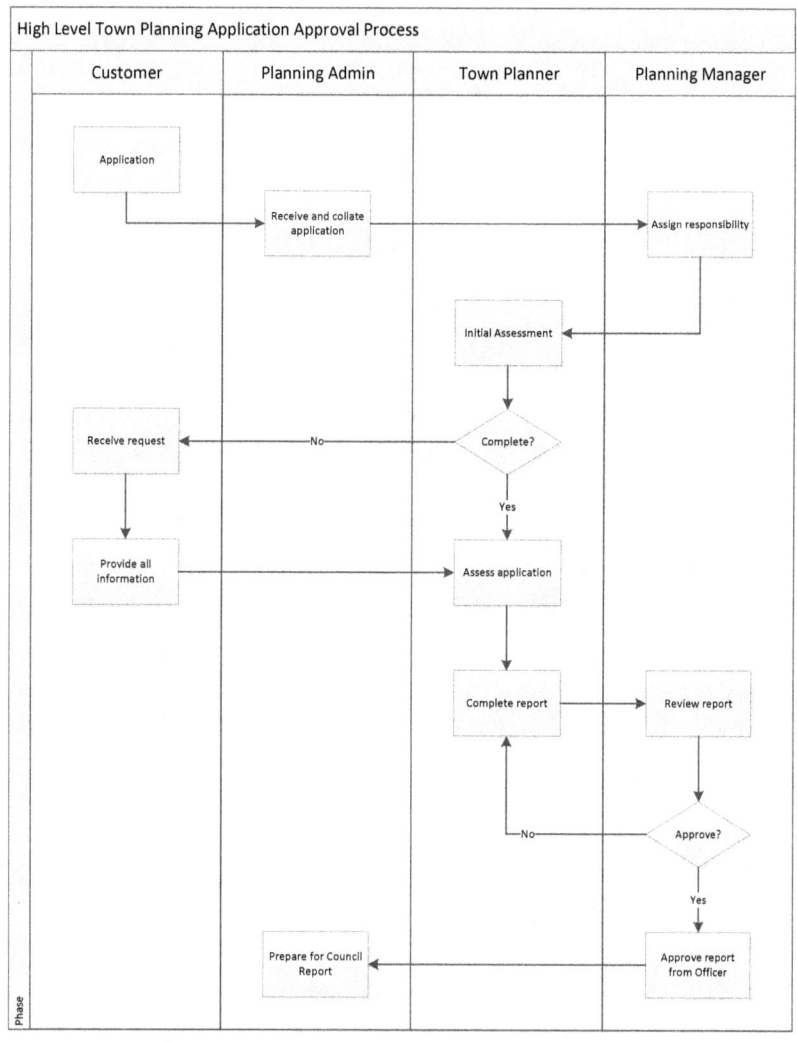

The above shows the worded process as a Deployment Flowchart or Process Map. As you can see, it is far easier to understand the process flow through the use of a process map. Now we have the process mapped it is time for the next step to a Value Stream Map, the process study.

Process Study

Put simply, a process study is used to capture the time taken to complete a process. An Excel template for completing a process study can be provided by emailing info@lean-learnings.com

So how does a process study work? To ensure the best data possible, ten cycles should be captured by three different operators or officers. This is a total of 30 applications, if the process volume is too low to enable this number of studies to be completed in a timely manner the number of cycles can be reduced or alternately, the number of officers can be reduced. If necessary I would adjust to measure five cycles with three officers which results in a total of 15 cycles.

The reason for capturing this spread of cycles is to ensure the final cycle time used in the Value Stream Map is a sound reflection of what is achievable and repeatable. When implementing standardized work you would normally use the lowest repeated time, I do not follow this method when using the process study for service as the variability in cycle times is often greater than for other process types, such as manufacturing. For a process study in service I use the average of the recorded times over the three officers. This will become clear as we go through the examples.

The process study becomes more of a challenge when we understand the process being measured. In the case of the Town Planning Application Process there is a high level of variability from application to application. This is managed by grouping the applications into a number of type groups. The number of type groups will depend on the variability and volume of each and will need to be determined for each specific process. Let's assume we have grouped the applications into four type groups; we will continue with group two.

How much detail should you go into when conducting the process study? Again, this varies greatly depending on the process itself; as a guide and general rule, the longer the total cycle time of the process the less detail the study. When studying a process with a short total cycle time it is necessary to go into greater detail as the savings per process steps are likely to be lower and by going into greater detail you will identify more waste that can be removed from the process. When the total process cycle time is greater there is likely to be more "low hanging fruit" or quick gains to be made. Remember this is not a one-time only activity and on subsequent activities the detail can and should increase through iterations.

Officer 1

Process Study	Process: Town Planning Application Approval - Initial Assessment						Observer: J Tisbury, Officer: John		Date/Time 10/02/2015		Process Study Number: 001

Process Steps	Block	Work Element	Observed Times					Repeatable / Average	Machine Cycle Time	Notes
			1	2	3	4	5			
1		Receive and collate application	45	37	41	30	35	37.6	■	
2		Assign responsibility	25	20	21	29	22	23.4	■	
3		Initial assessment	240	312	255	332	302	288.2	■	
4		Complete assessment	167	133	204	172	163	167.8	■	
5		Complete report	202	243	191	187	215	207.6	■	Includes reworking after Manager assessment
6		Approve report	67	74	59	80	77	71.4	■	Includes reworking after Officer rework
7		Prepare Council Report	114	95	107	132	99	109.4	■	

Officer 2

Process Study		Process: Town Planning Application Approval - Initial Assessment	Observer: J Tisbury Operators: Max					Date/Time: 17/02/2015		Process Study Number: 002
Process Steps	Block		Observed Times					Repeatable	Machine Cycle Time	Notes
			1	2	3	4	5			
1	Receive and collate application		51	56	48	61	41	51.4		
2	Assign responsibility		20	21	29	22	25	23.4		
3	Initial assessment		301	318	248	328	296	298.2		
4	Complete assessment		183	171	159	199	203	183		
5	Complete report		198	212	209	176	187	196.4		Includes reworking after Manager assessment
6	Approve report		71	77	65	79	70	72.4		Includes reworking after Officer rework
7	Prepare Council Report		102	89	98	112	121	104.4		

Officer 3

Process Study	Process: Town Planning Application Approval - Initial Assessment	Observer: J Tisbury Operators: Michelle		Date/Time: 21/02/2015		Process Study Number: 003

Process Steps	Block	Work Element	Observed Times					Repeatable	Machine Cycle Time	Notes
			1	2	3	4	5			
1		Receive and collate application	41	44	37	39	47	41.6		
2		Assign responsibility	31	27	25	29	24	27.2		
3		Initial assessment	312	331	297	301	287	305.6		
4		Complete assessment	199	176	169	181	142	173.4		
5		Complete report	198	171	206	179	168	184.4		Includes reworking after Manager assessment
6		Approve report	73	61	79	75	81	73.8		Includes reworking after Officer rework
7		Prepare Council Report	99	107	121	103	114	108.8		

As you can see, the above Process Studies are quite low in detail and are not difficult to complete. It is important to be an observer only and not interfere with the process being performed, aside from asking for the purpose of clarity for the completion of the study. In situations where the process is very unstable, this can be a difficult task to complete the study so a basic level of standardization is helpful; sometimes the first main action out of this activity is the basic standardization and that is a good step forward.

Process Flow Sheet

The next step is the Process Flow Sheet. This is a very common worksheet in manufacturing, however I believe it is just as useful in the service environment. The Process Flow Sheet is used to record the movement of the value item; in the case of the Town Planning application approval process, the value item is the application and subsequent report. It is easy to think that because we are not making anything, there is no material flow, this isn't true. Material can come in many different guises when we are discussing Value Streams; it can even be information and have absolutely no physical form!

Step	Flow	Dept.	Distance	Time	People
Receive and collate application	●	Admin		44 min	
	▽ ⇨			3 days	
Assign responsibility	⇨	Manager		25 min	
	▽ ⇨			7 days	
Initial assessment	●	Planner		298 min	
	▽ ⇨			20 days	
Complete assessment	●	Planner		175 min	
	▽ ⇨			5 days	
Complete report	●	Planner		197 min	
	▽ ⇨			5 days	
Approve report	●	Manager		73 min	
	▽ ⇨			3 days	
Prepare Council Report	●	Admin		108 min	

As you can see, the Process Flow Sheet is a combination of a couple of the previous documents. The addition of the "Flow" column helps us determine what is happening in the process and when it occurs.

Process Flow Sheet Legend

 Process

 Movement or transport

 Process stop

 Waiting

This information is important for the completion of the Value Stream Map in the next section.

You'll also notice the "Time" column and wonder where this figure came from as it different from those recorded on the Process Study. The values recorded on the Process Flow Sheet are:

- The average time recorded for each process study averaged out.

For example:

Receive and collate application:

Study 1:

The average of 45, 37, 41, 30, 35 is 38 (when rounded)

Study 2:

The average of 51, 56, 48, 61, 41 is 51

Study 3:

The average of 41, 44, 37, 39, 47 is 42

The average of 38, 51 and 42 is 44 which is the value recorded in the "Time" column.

Now you have the Process Map, Process Study and Process Flow Chart completed you have all the information you need to complete the Value Stream Map. Before you do though, it is a good idea to have the above documents reviewed by the team to check for any gaps or errors.

The Value Stream Map

There are a number of methods used to develop the VSM:

- There's the original paper and pencil using a roll of butcher's paper

- Some practitioners use sticky notes to both capture the data and develop the VSM

- Some use software programs like Microsoft Excel or Visio

- Others use purpose developed applications on computers or tablets

None of the above are right or wrong and all can work. The method doesn't really matter so I'm not going to preach on the benefits of one over the others. I will take you through the process I use to develop a VSM and you can decide on how you are going to going about it.

How I develop a Value Stream Map

1) The first thing I do, is complete all of the preceding steps. The level of detail of each step may vary depending on the size, complexity and maturity of the process being analyzed.

For example, if the process is immature, with little or no standard work in place, the initial study and map may not be in seconds. In some cases, the initial study hasn't even been in minutes or hours, but in days. This is because the work elements were so different from study one to study ten, to record the process was impossible. In this instance we measured at a lower detail level and the first kaizen was to standardize, before measuring again.

2) Setup a war room and post all of the work sheets on the wall. Post them in sequential order of the process, if possible on a single wall.

The war room is a room that can be left setup for the duration of the study. A meeting room can be used and is a good place as more people will be exposed to the study. I've seen some businesses keep it all secretive, I do not agree with this method; I believe the more people involved in and exposed to the study the better.

3) On a roll of butcher paper or on sheets of presentation paper hand draw the VSM with pencil. You can purchase stencils of the VSM icons, but I prefer to draw the entire thing by hand as it is faster. I'm not too bothered with how pretty it looks at this stage.

Starting with the supplier/s on the left, add the process steps from left to right. Place any parallel processes above or below the main value line. Where inventory is part of the current process, add the triangular icon and the inventory time.

4) Share with the team. Share the draft with the entire team and more if possible. The more questions and challenges you get through at this stage the easier the whole process will be.

Only once you've shared and reviewed should you take the next step.

5) Transfer the completed and reviewed VSM to Microsoft Visio. I do this for a couple of reasons.

A) Visio is a cleaner copy and makes presentation easier and clearer (especially with my messy handwriting) to others in the organization.

B) The Visio file can be saved as a PDF and emailed or shared much easier. This is very important for business units across multiple sites.

That's it, done! Ok, so now we'll go through the process of developing a simple VSM from the data we captured earlier.

The first thing is to add the supplier on the left hand side of the paper as below.

From the supplier add the process steps from left to right as shown in the below image.

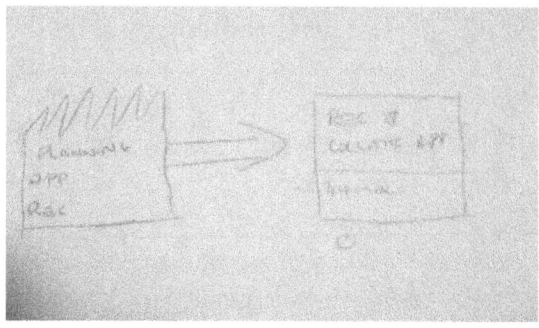

You will note the double lined arrow between the supplier and the first process. This is a push line and signifies the pushing of the application (product) through the process. The alternative is the pull arrow which is used when the product is pulled by demand through the process.

You'll also note process box is separated into two sections, the top half is the process name and the bottom half is the time to complete the step. This is taken from the process flow sheet. Under the process box, the small symbol indicates the number of operators or staff required to complete the task. For every step in this process, the number is one.

Where there is inventory or waiting between process steps, this is added with a triangular symbol.

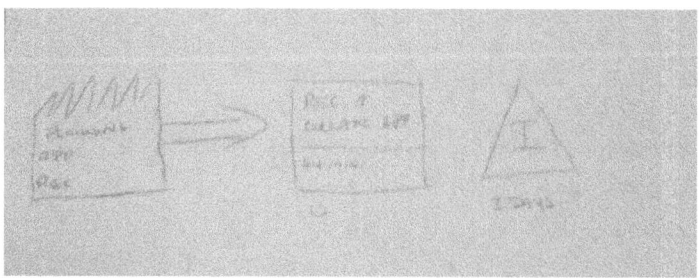

The number of days of inventory or waiting is recorded under the symbol.

Continue until the process is completed. Follow this with time line along bottom of page as in the below image.

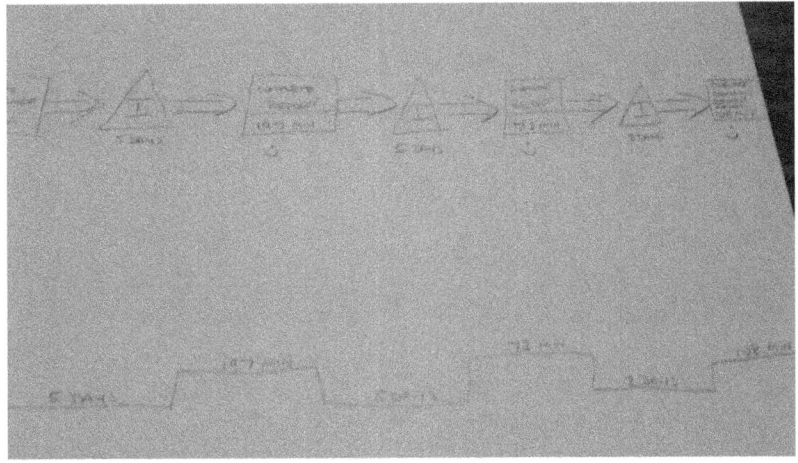

Finally, add the total cycle time and lead time data onto the VSM as below.

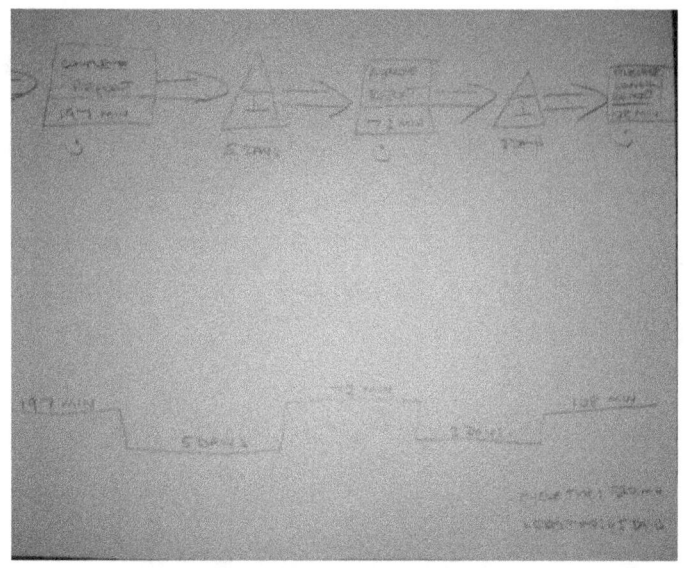

There you have it, a simple Value Stream Map. But what does it all mean? Let's break it all down.

The numbers that matter:

- Total lead time: 45 days

- Total cycle time: 920 minutes or two days

- 4.4% productive time

- 43 days waiting

43 days waiting out of 45 days lead time. It doesn't take much to figure out where the low hanging fruit is. We put our focus on the waiting time and reorganized the value stream into more of a pull system with the Planning Admin team being the internal customer "pulling" the application

through the process. We developed a simple spreadsheet to work as a scheduler and milestone tracker based on our new agreed timeframes.

I won't go into specific details here as to the agreed times or the spreadsheet as unless you are a Town Planner the information will not add value. A copy of the spreadsheet is available by emailing info@lean-learnings.com

By introducing a schedule (similar to a manufacturing schedule) into the process we were able to:

- Easily display due dates for completion of tasks

- Monitor adherence not only to overall on-time efficiency, but monitor the adherence to milestone delivery dates

- Ability to "pull" through the process. Let's take the "Approve report" step by the Manager as an example.

Before the changes, the manager would wait for a report to be submitted for approval by a planner. Remember, there may be ten or more planners; the waiting by the manager could quickly turn into waiting of the reports if multiple reports are handed in in quick succession. This would result in more delays for the process, and a big inbox for the manager.

After the changes the manager knows when every report is due to him by referring to the schedule. The manager can now plan for the report approval in their diary and "pull" the reports from the planners at the appropriate time. This will reduce waiting time for the manager, the planner, the application and will also greatly reduce the amount of reworking throughout the entire process.

A hidden benefit is the reduced rework; caused by the start/stop processing in the current state. Every time a person restarts a process from a stoppage, there is waste as they have to first review what has been completed to find where to restart from. In the case of the town planning application process this waste is more evident as the time between stops and starts can be quite some time. This results in even more waste in the restarting of the process.

This is just a single value stream map of a single process within a single government department. With the improvements that can be made by following the lean business principles in this one process, imaging what can be achieved when an entire government unit or an entire government takes on this journey!

6. Making the Changes Stick

It's all well and good to follow the example above and make some improvements, but how do you go about making it stick? And what about next steps?

Making it stick

In any business type, this is one of the most difficult steps of any improvement journey. When starting the journey, people are excited, enthusiastic and things get done; at least for a short time! It's no different in a government organization.

There are a number of steps you can take to give your journey the best chance of success and sustainability.

Recognition of efforts:

Recognising results is important, but it's just as important (especially in the early stages) to recognise the efforts of the team. Try to stay clear of holding individuals up on a pedestal; remember this is all about culture and you don't want to promote a culture of star individuals, you want a culture of high performing teams.

Recognition can be as simple as a poster showing the before and after journey.

Celebration:

It's been mentioned a number of times already, but a celebration is a great way to promote the efforts of a team and to give a reward. Make sure the scale of the celebration is relative to the achievements. Don't go all out with a great celebration after a sort session (remember 5S); and don't give a small celebration after achieving a major milestone KPI.

Recognizing and celebrations will only go so far though towards making the journey sustainable; the best way to achieve sustainability is to be consistently engaged. That may sound easy, however you cannot fake it; you will be caught out. You simply cannot be consistent if you're faking it.

To be consistent means to walk the walk every day; we all have off days, and this is the only time it's ok to fake it, just to get you through. How do you get the whole team to be consistent? This is your role as a manager; it is your role to create and share the vision for your team to chase and want to be a part of. This is where we create the culture and culture is what makes it all stick; culture makes or breaks a sustainable journey.

So how do you go about creating this culture? Well there is no one thing you need to do, and it is a different answer for different businesses and business types; Government is no different there…

However as with everything else, there is a process that can be followed.

Step 1) Set the scene

This is where we develop the vision, mission and values of your team and is the first stage of business planning. We discussed this in an earlier chapter so will not go into too much now; however it must be reiterated the importance of this being developed with and by the team, at least the senior members of the team. This should not be your vision alone.

Make your vision something worth chasing; it needs to be inspirational, otherwise why would anyone bother joining you on the journey? Being a part of many government departments has become a boring prospect, we need to appeal to the best of the best to improve the bloodlines so to speak. We can only do this by creating a vision worth chasing.

Step 2) Share the dream

A team can have the best vision in the world, but if the vision is not shared it will amount to nothing. Sharing does not simply mean to put a poster in the foyer; sharing a vision is a process in itself.

Sharing the vision is all about engagement of the team. When you share the vision through engagement, you are developing a team rather than just giving instructions. A shared vision will result in:

- Everyone working towards a common goal
- True productivity, working on what matters rather than just keeping busy
- Purposeful work with engaged community

When you share the vision effectively, everyone will have the same view of what the end result looks like.

Step 3) Build a plan

Again, this was largely discussed in an earlier chapter. Planning how you and your team will achieve the vision is a critical step. The old adage "failing to plan is planning to fail" is very true in all aspects.

Break the plan down into roles, so everyone knows the part they play and how what they do on a day to day basis brings the team closer to achieving its goals. This is a key point, what motivates people is knowing they are a part of something bigger than themselves.

Step 4) Measure

The key to a strong successful team is measurement and analysis. It's important to measure what really matters; this can sometimes be a challenge as the results are not always positive. Don't be a team that only measures the good outcomes; in reality, measuring what you are good at is somewhat of a waste. If you cannot make a decision, or learn something from the results you are measuring the wrong things.

You will find a free KPI setup tool on our website.

Step 5) Break the government typecast

This one may be a little controversial with many government employees. There is a typecast of the government employee being disengaged, lazy and largely non-value adding. We've all seen the jokes, if you haven't, just search for 'government worker jokes' on the internet.

As this typecast is widespread (across continents), it will be difficult to break. We can all do our bit though.

Within your own team, strive to be the most successful team in your department. That's somewhere to start. You see, from my experience within government organizations, success is something that is not strived for; it's almost taboo! This is what we need to break.

Remember the customer! They are also the community in many cases. Just because you are not working for a business where profits are a key objective doesn't mean the customer is any less important. Saying that, you don't have to be a social justice proponent to engage in government work either. Just like any business, it takes all types for a team to be successful.

Be aware of the typecast and be above it. Don't be afraid to stand out from the crowd and succeed.

Step 6) Repeat what works well

Through the measurement towards your goals, you will find some things work well and others not so well. One of the roles of a manager is to identify what it is that you and your team are doing well; why are you achieving some of your goals and not others? Take what is working well, take it apart to understand why and see where and how you can apply it to other areas that perhaps are not doing quite as well.

Bring your teams into these discussions, don't try and work this all out by yourself. They know what works; together you can figure out why and turn it into a process; this is how all processes are created.

7. Common Failings

As an almost final word, I am going to give a few of my personal experiences from working in a government organization. These are given to share the culture from an outsider's point of view. These views were gained after spending a number of years working and consulting to the private sector and are made as a comparison to some best practices found in a number of other industries.

In no way are these comments meant to embarrass or be demeaning to anyone. These are just the behaviours and values I witnessed while working within the government environment. There are no names or places for the purpose of anonymity. Not surprisingly, many of these are antonyms of much of what was discussed in chapter 6.

Lack of engagement

This is a common issue in all business types, but is commonly observed in government organizations. Most employees start off with good engagement, however over time the engagement level drops due to any number of factors. This is what I call a Principal Culture Failure; Principal because it sits at the top of the reasons why a person leaves a job (either physically or mentally); Culture because it is very rarely a single employee that disengages. Many of the following are in fact causes of this Principal Culture Failure; I see the PCF as the effect.

Being a PCF, many of the following examples are in fact strongly related to and contribute to this symptom. In the government sector it is a real shame when an employee loses their engagement because it is a lose / lose situation. Studies show actively disengaged employees cost the U.S. economy in excess of $500 billion in lost productivity each year. This is a commercial figure and does not automatically translate to the government sector, however shows the impact this PCF can have on business.

As I've said a number of times in these pages, many people join a government organization not only as a job, but as a way to give service to their community. When they become disengaged they lose their passion for what they are doing. As it is human nature to perform better when we're engaged, it makes sense that when their engagement reduces, the quality of work also reduces resulting in a lower service provided to the very community the employee wanted to serve when they joined.

Very rarely, is a lack of engagement the fault of the employee; very, very rarely. It is a direct result of poor management and leadership as the following causes will show.

Poor management communication

"We talk a lot, but we don't communicate" is one of my favorite sayings and is another common issue found in all business types. If this is a problem in your government organization don't think you're alone. According to PDP Solutions, a study by Towers Watson showed businesses with highly effective internal communications had 47%

higher returns. Imagine what this translates to in servicing the community!

We all spend a lot of time and even money on external communication, but internal communications are sadly under-resourced yet play an increasing part in organizational performance.

I've spoken a lot in these pages about business planning, well here is a little more. Any business plan should include an internal communications plan which starts from the organization chart. Forget about people, we need to look at the roles in the organization and particularly the level they sit within the organization. Some people take a bit of offence to the acknowledgement of hierarchical levels within an organization, but the reality is they do exist and they need to exist so we may as well be honest with ourselves and acknowledge them.

An internal communication plan looks at each level and the roles in the organization and attempts to clearly define what this role needs to be informed of, when and how the communication should be made for best outcomes. I also like to add an assessment for why, or what is the expectation for what the role will do with this information. Are they expected to make a decision? It may just be for information purposes only. It is important to make this assessment to ensure the right level of detail is provided to the recipient.

Below is an example of a simple internal communications plan template. An Excel version is available on our website.

Communication (What)	Level	Role	Purpose (Why)	Method (How)

Lack of accountability

This is a big one! This is one of the most complained about issues when it comes to staff engagement. Not all managers should be in management positions.

The major reason this is an issue is managers do not know how to do their jobs! Sorry to be direct, but this is a big frustration of mine. As long as businesses continue to promote their best technical experts to the position of manager this will continue to be an issue. We have forgotten what a manager is for; the position of manager is not about remunerating our best technical experts better, the position of manager is there to manage the value stream, lead the team and meet organizational targets and objectives.

In the search to better remunerate our technical experts we promote them to manager. This does no-one any favors. These technical experts are not necessarily management material; this results in poor team cohesion. I don't believe it is necessary for a manager to have high technical expertise at all; what is important is that the manager is a skilled people leader.

The only way to develop accountability is to set clear individual work-plans that are:

- Fairly and equally developed across the team
- Agreed with the team member
- Cascading of the teams accountabilities and responsibilities – more on this next
- Measurable

The lower performing the team, the more frequently these need to be reviewed with the individuals. I also share the high level plans with the entire team. I find this can promote improved team work when done with the right mindset. Don't do this if your intention is to embarrass low performers or to promote the efforts of high achievers; this should be a team building exercise.

A reminder, promoting for longevity of service or technical prowess is not good for sustainable growth.

No link between work and strategic objectives

This one was mentioned earlier and is another regularly seen issue. There is possibly nothing less engaging than putting your efforts towards nothing. No matter who we are or where we fit into the organization, we all work better and are more engaged when we know our efforts are helping to achieve something bigger.

One of the main characteristics and strengths of a good leader is the ability to "share the dream". Whether you call it the vision, the strategy or the targets and objectives; it amounts to the same thing, the reason why we are all here!

107

Sharing this with your team and empowering your team to play their part in achieving the success is a gift that I don't believe can be easily learned. One can however learn how to share the strategy through individual and team work-plans though. While this may not have the romance or drama of a visionary leader, it can be a very effective method of creating a high performing team.

On our website www.mlbc.com.au you will find a template I use for sharing the strategic plan both with the team and the individuals within the team.

Confusing or conflicting priorities

Lastly for this section we have confusing or conflicting priorities. Knowing and having a work plan linked to the strategic plan can be empowering, however if you are still working on menial tasks that are conflicting with the strategy it can be torturous for any employee.

In any organization there are a many tasks that may appear menial, but if the work in any way brings the group closer to the goals then the work is linked to the strategy. If the work of any employee does not bring the group closer to the goals, then this work by nature is waste. This is where this all ties into the lean government vision; if the work of any worker does not a) bring direct value to the community, or b) bring the group closer to its goals or strategy then the work is waste and should be reviewed or removed altogether.

8. Final Word

I thank-you for taking the time out to read this guide and I truly hope you have found at least some help within the pages. Working in a government organization can be a greatly rewarding and greatly frustrating experience simultaneously and I thank you for giving your time to help your community.

This guide has been written from my personal experiences and comparisons of my time working in and with government, private and public organizations. On a personal note, I have found working with government organizations an interesting, if not contradictory experience.

On the one hand, there are so many individuals doing their best to give something to and to provide the best service they can to their community. Whilst at the same time, the very organizations created to provide these much needed services develop so much waste (of both resources and money).

The purpose of writing this guide is to open the minds within these government organizations to see the waste. Nothing can be done if we cannot see the problem; this is always the very first step.

www.ingramcontent.com/pod-product-compliance
Lightning Source LLC
Chambersburg PA
CBHW070050210526
45170CB00012B/636